The Rhyming Kind

A Book of Rookie Poems

Kayt Gary

BookLeaf Publishing
India | USA | UK

Made with ❤ on the BookLeaf Publishing Platform
www.bookleafpub.in
www.bookleafpub.com

Dedication

To anyone who told me they like
my poems.
In honesty or in pity.

Preface

Written in 21 days
Some in Amsterdam,
Some in Morocco,
Some in Belgium
But all in love
For better or for worse.

Acknowledgements

Thanks to Laurens van Cleef for listening to the work in progress and making me the best ramen in the world to fuel my creativity.

Thanks to Lucas Jones and Harry Baker for just being amazing. You are my two favorite (famous) poets.

Thanks to MKS for the encouragement and content inspiration.

1. Amsterdam

There once was a blonde from the States
Who preferred dirty martinis on dates
Sought her love in a city
To discover the pity
Europe only serves olives on plates

2. Dilemma

Is there room for me in that heart of yours
Or is she still hiding behind your door
Am I wishing for something that doesn't exist
Is it foolish of me to still persist
Was I the only one who felt that spark
Or has that light always been dark
Is this distance making your heart grow fonder
Or should I let my eyes go wander

3. Miles

Maybe it's a little bit selfish
I want to reach my arm around the globe and touch your heart
Put my hand on your chest and heal it
I wish I could brush away the pain
So you didn't have to feel it.
I would press fast forward and rewind all at the same time
To somehow get her off your mind
Not to erase her, just to chase her out
So you could find peace
So your joy returns, you see the light
and your heart has room to breathe.

Maybe it's a little bit selfish
To want your wound to heal a little faster
So you feel a little less of a disaster
and want to play again.
So when you tie your shoes and run again,
Your legs don't feel so heavy.
So every turn your not expecting something to remind you
of what is no longer
Instead you see new colors

You discover streets you've never taken
The colors seem brighter, your steps a bit lighter
and you start to run again.

Maybe it's a little selfish
But its the first time in a while
I've overthought every text
Wondered when I'd see you next
Whose hand in mine is sweaty
and I'm nervous and can't seem to wipe this silly grin from my face
It's been a while since I've felt that place
That little place inside my heart that's been shut awhile
Gathered dust waiting for something worthwhile

Maybe it's a little selfish
Maybe it's a little to soon and not usually my style
But I've been running through these miles
And I can tell you its the first time in a long time
I've been running with a smile.

4. You Pick

I like that one, not this one
That one's too small
I'm afraid if I commit
I'll miss out on all

So I look and I scan
I test and I try
But no more than that
I just say goodbye

I wait and I wish
Till one catches my eye
I think I spotted him
I'm so happy I cry

5. Not My Best Work

Are we really all that different
or are we all just the same
If our struggles were so unique to us
Who am I playing in this game?
They said if I didn't win today
Tomorrow'd be a brighter day
are we all just faking it
Because it feels just the same.
Today I woke up with a feeling oh so blue
The people I thought I loved, hardly even knew
Did all those people yesterday wake up and play today?
Did they get up or give up and simply walk away?
The game must have ended or maybe it's my turn
It feels so familiar, maybe a lesson I didn't learn
But I play it anyway, what else is there to do?
Deny my heart and hide from it,
Fake it till I'm through?
Did you win today?
Will you play tomorrow?
Have you been feeling blue?
Does the game ever end
Or are you pretending too?

6. Green Skies & Blue Grass

Maybe you met fate on a date with another guy
A brief conversation , something gentle in his eyes
you brushed it off, you heard he'd been with her for quite some time
And the guy you were with kinda felt ... not bad, he was fine
But that something in his eyes sorta stuck in your mind
You didn't look or dig and a few months go by
You mention to your friend one day on a run
Out of the blue you really aren't sure why
You ask sorta shyly about that cute guy
Funny timing, she mentions the breakup a little surprised
She really hurt him, he had quite on the line
You brush it off, realizing the timings not right
Plus what are the odds he's even your type
Then New Years Eve your worlds collide
You skin and you smile and you talk for a while
He's funny and kind
There's something about him not like other guys
But the timings not right his heart needs space
So unpatiently you wait, reel it in and try save face
Each time you see him your suspicion confirmed
but the silence between you is starting to burn

And you should brush it off, meet someone new
But he's stitched in the fibers way too tight to undo
So before you leave you try one last time
Then just like that his hand is sweaty in yours
Making up games and tallying scores
Stealing him away, being shushed by the crowd
For talking too loud they hate that
Youre in your own world where the grass is blue
And skies are green and you're over the moon
His arm is asleep because you won't move
But he leaves it there just for you
You can't sleep you wish you could stay
Forever like that so many things you can't say
What if you met fate when everything you thought you loved
Broke your heart and walked away?

7. Politics

There once was a coin worth one cent
Almost worthless whenever it was spent
It brought luck to the many
Trump cancelled the penny
And with it their good fortune went

8. My Favorite

I like square plates
I like the color yellow
and stories to animate
I like the smell of old books
Riding horses and picking hooves
I like waking up early
like so insanely early before the world wakes up
when the light is gentle on the trees
the air is quiet before time speeds up
I like chocolate
like a lot of chocolate,
One might say a chocoholic
its probably my favorite
maybe an addiction so don't enable it
I like receiving mail
all mail even bills
the fact that someone somewhere took time to send me something
the old school way, melts my heart a little
I like riding hills
like moving so slowly you're almost standing still
every muscle working to take you just a little higher
my legs are on fire and I like fire
the disappearing act of flames is mesmorizing

the beauty and destruction equalizing
I like the smell of burning ditches
it will forever remind me of Grandma Mary Gary
sending boats under irrigation stream bridges
I like shuffling cards, I learned at her house and
all the card houses we used to build thousands
and we'd pile up leaves, climb up the trees and jump till
we sleep
out of all my childhood memories, I treasure these
I like being in my own world
airpods in, my hair whirled by the wind
I feel like I'm in a music video
getting lost amongst the city folk
I like the color pink
Not to wear on clothes and things
but how nature does it
Like God spared no expense and blew the budget
Just to dazzle us with painted pinks
I like gold rings
and silver
but right now gold is in my quiver
I like the way the air sparkles
at -32 degrees celcius
its remarkable
I liked writing this list
I could go on for days but
you get the gist

so i'll leave you with that
oh, and one more thing --
I love your hat

9. Happy

Today I met a happy thought
It woke me up with a wild plot
Whispered in my ear
The secret to not fear
Is simply opting to fear not

10. Gambling

We made a bet that day to see who could guess
How much that deer weighed-- one hundred fifty at best?
No way you said five hundred! boldly without doubt
I didn't really care who won, just happy to hangout
But just to set the record straight, I definitely had that one

11. Connected

Scars are journal entries
Etched in our skin
The evidence of wounds
We healed from within

A token reminder
that this to shall pass
A token reminder
We found healing at last

The deeper the wound
The better story it tells
of making it through
What then felt like hell

Each one unique
Yet one thing the same
Our stories are ours
But we all know the pain

12. Road Less Traveled

I am my following footsteps father
Decisions I made started digging my grave
But these footloose feet couldn't be bothered

If people with out problems were dead
Rules broke what it meant to be alive
and I tried to catch even death by surprise

Unsustainably thrilling but the thrill failed to fulfill
and when the pendulum swung, it hit like a drill
realizing living large wasn't apart of something larger

To continue this way was just pushing me farther
I had it all backwards and a little mixed up
all along it was discipline, freedom had in her cup

13. Blondie

There once was a ginger in Belgium
She felt her hair was unwelcome
She went to a salon
but the blonde went wrong
and now has to wait to shed some

14. Pops

Your father always said you can be anything you please
And he believed it-- a doctor, a lawyer, an astronaut--
can you see it?
He'd look at you and say it so many times you can't
count
Apart of your worldview it was layered throughout

Your father always said be slow to anger and work your
tail off
When it gets under your skin shake it off; trust me, it
pays off

Like he stayed, he paid his dues to support you through
All your mind could dream up, all your mind could think
of
Were his words, when you wanted to pause and give up

So you picked a job, nothing special, just entry level
You stayed, you paid your dues and shook off the feeling
It wasn't quite right but you kept on believing in the goal
you're achieving

It's a great opportunity, his words playing so loud
You've climbed so high and you're making him proud

You'd be crazy to leave now; just keep your chin up
Hard work isn't easy, be grateful and buck up

All of a sudden 11 years have gone by since you've felt
like yourself,
The real you is collecting dust somewhere on a shelf
You don't remember the last time you felt joy
To fit the new box you now want to destroy

Then one day you wake up, crippled with fear
With your nose on the grindstone for too many years
The path you took isn't quite where you belong
You doubt your fathers words was he wrong all along?

Then it hits you like a ton of rocks
What he was trying to say in all those long talks
What you want you can have, so don't ever quit it
The world is your oyster my daughter, you have no limit

15. Paths

There once was a poet sweet on the ears
But she chose accounting to be her career
The longer she counted
It drew from her fountain
and no one has heard her words in years

16. Illusion

You're feeling lost a little, Child
In a forest of big trees
You've been running quite a while now
Their success is all you see

You might not have the feeling
The envy made you numb
It has robbed your memory
Of battles that you won

Don't measure the endeavor
By the glow of the horizon
You'll be chasing it forever
Blinded by comparison

So give yourself some credit, Child
Look how far you've run
For that's a better measure
To see how far you've come

17. Ode to Bob

We've gone a thousand miles in Morocco
Lost on the roads so many go down
Its a colorful world full of deserts and trees
Of hustlers and parrots and rugs and mint tea

Hi hi Chrissy Ford I wrote you this poem
About things I see that I'm comin to know
Your curious and driven steadfast never torn
It seems like a skeptic since the day you were born

Your patient and calm when I'm challenging you
And all the control you take when you do
Here's to the way you see life's mysteries
The standards you hold for yourself and all things

It took me a while to say the words in this way
I didn't know how so I sat there and prayed
It hit me so hard I knew what to do
Is to find the beauty in these things about you

So now the things that are easier to say
That you my dear friend are alive here today
I thank the Designer and you thank design
but as long as you're here all that matters is fine

Hi hi Chrissy Ford I'm sorry you know
For lately the troubles you've seen on your road
You've been broken and bruised and shaken to the bone
I'm here my friend, don't carry your burden alone

18. Disclaimer

What you're reading are my thoughts
That I wrote without fear
The first of many had to start here

I accepted a challenge
On a whim of some sorts
A few of them long, but most of them short

You'll see errors throughout
So don't look too close
It makes it seem more authentic I suppose

Hesitate no further
And enjoy some laughs
I need to get back to analyzing graphs

19. Disclaimer part 2

Oh I forgot, a couple more things
You'll probably notice a few of my themes

There's a boy who I like
Not sure if he likes me
Then one about Morocco
With my friend, her name is Chrissy

I'm living in Amsterdam
So I wrote one about that,
Lots of discovering I'm on the wrong path

My dad, or Pops as I like to call him
Is in a few of them too
If you have never met him,
be sure that you do

The final theme is weaved throughout
One that some of you might doubt

And that is happiness
I think it's a choice
It will change the game, just give it a voice

That sums it up
I'll let you go now goodbye
Thanks for reading and enjoy your time

20. Ending comments

That's it, that's a wrap
The ending has come
I hope you enjoyed
It was tons of fun

21. Ending comments Part 2

The funny thing about this challenge
Is it lasted a brief three weeks
Which sounds like a lot, but it felt like a squeeze

Some days I was in a flow
and others felt like pulling teeth
some words obvious, others deeper underneath

the funny thing about this challenge
is how imperfectly it all will look
but exactly what I needed to jumpstart my next book

www.ingramcontent.com/pod-product-compliance
Lightning Source LLC
Chambersburg PA
CBHW051751130826
49812CB00033B/1098
* 9 7 8 9 3 7 0 9 2 4 6 4 2 *